Collector's Guide to

Country

Baskets

Don & Carol Raycraft

COLLECTOR BOOKS

A Division of Schroeder Publishing Co., Inc.

The current values in this book should be used only as a guide. They are not intended to set prices, which vary from one section of the country to another. Auction prices as well as dealer prices vary greatly and are affected by condition as well as demand. Neither the Author nor the Publisher assumes responsibility for any losses that might be incurred as a result of consulting this guide.

The bear on the back cover is a 1982 Steiff Commemorative. The heart on page 3 is a contemporary basket of grape vines.

Photography:
Carol Raycraft
Bob and Judy Farling
Lee and Cindy Sawyer
R. Craig Raycraft
Howard Bush

We appreciate the contributions of the following to this project:

Lee and Cindy Sawyer, Blue Bucket Antiques, Virginia Beach, Va.
Bob and Judy Farling
Chris Farling
Opel and Joe Pickens
Rev. Alex Hood, Quito, Ecuador
Mrs. John Hardy
Bill Schroeder
Steve Quertermous
Debbie Kern
Stewart Salowitz
Ryan C. Tucker
Robert A. Wills

INTRODUCTION

People have collected American furniture, pottery, and textiles for more than a century. Searching diligently through dusty shops, sun drenched outdoor shows, and barely lighted basements for handcrafted splint baskets is a relatively new phenomenon.

Prior to the 1970's, baskets were seldom advertised or prominently displayed in shops. At farm auctions, baskets were often thrown into a single lot and offered for whatever a misinformed bidder would pay.

There is a tendency for the demand for particular facets of the antiques market to dramatically rise and fall in direct relation to what is being featured in the current country-oriented home furnishing magazines. If a house that is photographed has a unique collection of cookie cutters, the national demand for them suddenly increases and prices rise.

It is our considered opinion that several magazine articles that appeared in the early 1970's, which displayed beamed ceilings filled with splint baskets, might have ignited the initial demand for country baskets. We saw a Pennsylvania stone house that had been restored and furnished with painted furniture and a beamed ceiling loaded with baskets. Shortly after the publication of the article, we became serious collectors of country baskets. There is little doubt that many other collectors followed the same path to potential poverty and frequent frustration.

It in unlikely that you will find a Pennsylvania dower chest or a heavily decorated Bennington crock in a roadside shop in Iowa that specializes in Depression glass and used books. It *is* within the realm of possibility that an uncommon basket form used on a nearby farm passed into the shop's possession through an estate or farm sale. Dealers who don't specialize in American country antiques often underreact or overreact to a piece with which they are not familiar and price it accordingly. It may not automatically be a bargain, but it might be a great basket.

Baskets were used throughout the nineteenth century for a variety of purposes in all parts of the nation. They were locally produced by part-time basket makers who sold their wares inexpensively or bartered them for other goods or services. The market for handcrafted "working" baskets was almost non-existent by 1900. Factory-made splint baskets machine-cut to precise sizes and sold cheaply made it impossible for country basketmakers to laboriously gather and prepare their materials and produce their ware at a profit. Paper bags, metal containers, and the mass marketed baskets forced the country basketmakers to seek other avenues of employment.

Country baskets were functional and were not designed to be decorative. When a bottom was broken out of a field basket or a handle was snapped, the basket was usually discarded or used for kindling. Relatively few nineteenth or early twentieth century baskets have survived and current prices reflect that scarcity.

This particular volume is primarily focused on "working" baskets rather than "fancy" baskets. "Working" baskets were usually constructed to carry out a specific function. "Working" baskets were not admired, treasured, and displayed for their beauty like "fancy" baskets. They were used each day to make life simpler and more convenient.

The Shakers produced both types of baskets. Their "fancy" baskets were made of woven poplar that was processed by machine. The baskets were sold for storing jewelry and enhancing a mail-ordered Victorian bedroom.

"Fancy" baskets were also manufactured for Easter and May Day celebrations. The non-Shaker "fancy" baskets that have survived generally have minimal value to collectors.

A "golden age" for many "fancy" basket collectors occurred between the Centennial Exposition of 1876 and the First World War. During this period of almost fifty years the Arts and Crafts Movement made a dramatic impact on the life styles of many Americans. "Lost" skills such as basket making, furniture making with hand tools, and quilting suddenly became fashionable again. The Arts and Crafts Movement was a reaction to the rise of factories and mass produced products for the home.

Most of the baskets made during this period were designed to demonstrate the maker's individual skill and flair for design. Basket making became an art form and raffia, rice-straw, sweet grass, cane, and honeysuckle vine were used rather than the white oak, ash, willow, and hickory used by maker's of "working" baskets.

A major difficulty in collecting country baskets is attempting to ascertain their age. A century old basket was made from the same type of raw materials and with similar weaving techniques as baskets produced by contemporary crafts people. Exposure to soil, water, sun, and the weather can prematurely age a basket fifty years in a single year. Similar basket forms have also been used for more than a century and this makes dating individual examples with any degree of accuracy especially difficult.

Scholars have determined that baskets were being made in the American Southwest almost ten thousand years ago. Even at that point it probably took the basket maker longer to find, gather, and prepare his splint than it did to create the basket form.

COUNTRY BASKETS

Painted utility or all-pupose basket, 15″ diameter, yellow interior and blue green exterior, possibly Shaker-made, New England, nineteenth century.

Oak splint storage basket, painted green with earlier coat of red underneath, rectangular base with an oval mouth or top, 16″ end to end and 4″ deep.

The bottom of the basket was woven in an open weave or checker work pattern.

It took a talented basket maker to combine an oval mouth with a square or rectangular bottom.

The checker work or plaited bottoms of three of these baskets were completed with a simple over and under weaving pattern. The open weave was commonly used on storage baskets because it allowed any moisture or water to run off and some air to circulate within the basket.

A wide variety of rims and bindings were also utlitzed. A rim could be "single" wrapped with splint or "double" wrapped for additional strength. Double wrapping was also called "x" binding. Each of these baskets has a double rim.

Unusual splint knife and fork basket, painted, 11″ long x 6½″ wide x 5″ deep, checker work bottom, New England, late nineteenth century. The carved bow handle was notched into the double rim of the basket.

Utility or vegetable gathering basket, southeastern United States, early twentieth century, factory-made of machine cut splint, painted. The basket would have minimal value if it was not covered with "old" paint.

Tightly woven buttocks basket, oak splint, worn green paint.

Utility basket, machine cut splint, thick oak splint handle, early twentieth century, covered with a red "wash". A "wash" is a mixture of paint and water that is thin enough to allow the grain of the splint to show through.

Oak splint garden basket, carved handle, painted, ca. late nineteenth century.

An assortment of turn-of-the-century country baskets.

Oak splint utility basket, possibly Shaker-made, New England, nineteenth century, 12″ across and 13½″ high to top of carved splint handle. The orange or bittersweet paint used on this basket makes it an exceptional example.

Storage or utility basket, painted weavers, probably Algonkian or Iroquois Indian-made, 7″ long, 5″ wide x 4″ deep, checker work construction, late nineteenth century.

It would not be uncommon for this basket to also have been decorated with a stenciled "potato" stamp.

Indian-made storage basket, 7″ deep x 17″ across, oak splint, curicue or "curly" decoration, probably New England, early twentieth century.

Checker work bottom and skillfully notched bow handle.

Finely made storage basket, oak splint, blue print, ca. nineteenth century, checker work bottom.

The bow handles on this basket and the thinly cut oak splint would not support a great deal of weight. The basket was probably made for use on a table or bureau.

This basket measures 10″ long x 6″ across x 4″ high.

Oak splint cheese or curd basket, New England, nineteenth century.

The basket measures only 13" across. The basket was placed over a crock and a piece of cheese cloth was placed inside. A mixture of curds and whey was poured into the cloth and the basket. The curds remained in the cloth and the whey went through the cloth and into the crock. The whey was then fed to the pigs.

Uncommonly well-made Shaker cheese basket, found in New York State, ca. nineteenth century, oak splint, 14″ diameter.

Cheese baskets can be found with diameters up to 30″. The miniature cheese baskets (12″-14″) are found less often.

Windsor-type cheese ladder, oak, mid-nineteenth century, New England, 26″ diameter. This is a variation of a cheese basket that had the "cheese ladder" already attached. The "ladder" was placed on the crock with the cloth and basket on top.

Pine "cheese" ladder, nailed together, ca. nineteenth century.

"Cheese" weave drying basket, possibly Shaker-made, New England, nineteenth century. The open weave construction allowed herbs to dry easily while being stored in the basket. Occasionally this form is misidentified and sold as cheese basket. A routine inspection of the finely cut splint would indicate that the basket could not hold up to the wear a cheese basket would be expected to endure.

Painted oak splint basket, possibly made as a gift, found in New York State, ca. mid-nineteenth century, 7½″ high to top of handle, 5″ diameter.

The handle was carved from a piece of oak splint and notched to the rim. This is an exceptional country basket.

Market basket, uncommon form, blue weavers for decoration, oak splint, carved handle.

Classic example of machine-cut splint basket, wide oak splint, probably sold filled with produce, twentieth century. Each weaver is the same because they were machine cut to an exact width and length.

Storage basket, never had a handle, probably Indian-made, late nineteenth century, multicolored dyed weavers.

Oak splint buttocks basket, colored weavers at base, thick oak handle, late nineteenth-early twentieth century.

The basket was tightly woven and the handle was carefully reinforced.

Storage basket used for holding produce on a table, oak splint, dyed weavers, splayed sides to 14″ x 14″ mouth, carved bow handles.

The bottom of the basket is checker worked or plaited with thick, oak splint.

Drop or swing handled basket, great blue paint, reinforced bottom, oak splint, found in New Hampshire, ca. nineteenth century, 12″ to the top of the handle and 10″ diameter.

Nest of four swing handled baskets made by contemporary maker Loren Holland of New York State.

The "x" bound or double wrapped rim is a technique commonly used by country basket makers.

Exposure to sunlight, air, and wear over time will give this checker work bottom a patina that could easily fool the next generation of collectors.

Early swing handled basket, New Hampshire origin, turned wooden bottom, 17½" tall, 14½" diameter at mouth, oak splint.

Nantucket, Massachusetts "light-ship" basket, rib construction, rattan, turned pine bottom, swing handle, ca. late nineteenth-early twentieth century.

The turned pine bottom, rattan or cane weavers imported from the Phillipines or China, swing handle, and rib construction are the distinguishing characteristics of the basket form that originated on the South Shoal Lightship off Nantucket Island.

Take special note of the single wrapped rim and the turnings on the inside of the basket.

Adaptation of the Nantucket in a contemporary basket by Mr. Holland.

This signed and dated basket was made with white oak rather than rattan.

Swing handled splint basket, found in New England, nineteenth century, 12″ diameter and 14″ to top of handle.

Swing handled oak splint basket, 10″ diameter and 12″ to top of handle. A swing handled basket without major breaks in the splint would be difficult to find for less than $200.00.

Oak splint swing handled basket, late nineteenth century, turned wooden bottom, 14″ diameter, rim wrapped with unusually wide piece of splint.

The carved oak handle is held to the basket by the bows. The bow is fit between the double rim and notched to hold it securely.

Miniature swing handled basket, possibly Shaker-made, oak splint, woven over a mold, nineteenth century, 5″ diameter, 8″ to top of handle.

A basket that was designed to carry eggs or produce occasionally can be found with a demi-john or "kicked up" bottom. This allowed the contents of the basket to be evenly distributed around its sides. The miniature buttocks has a raised, "kicked up", or demi-john bottom.

This is the interior of a storage basket with a demi-john bottom.

A great deal of workmanship was involved in the weaving of a country basket. The bottom of this basket was designed to provide balance and stability when it was placed on a table or counter.

Reinforced bottom on an oak splint basket.

The handle on this contemporary swing handled basket is held by a copper rivet rather than a hand carved bow.

White oak splint basket, swing or drop handle, round mouth with squared bottom, found in New England, ca. late nineteenth century.

The bows of the basket are inserted through the double rim, notched, and held in place by the weavers.

The "runners" on the checker worked bottom of the basket serve as braces and also protect the splint from wasting away.

Shaker double swing handled market basket, copper rivets anchor handles, single wrapped rim, 21½″ x 12″ x 15½″ to top of handles, New England, nineteenth century.

Shaker miniature basket, ash splint, woven over a mold, New England, ca. late nineteenth century, made for sale to the "world", 5″ diameter x 6″ to top of the handle. The Shakers had small shops in many of their Eastern communities where they sold sewing kits, boxes, carriers, cloaks, postcards, and baskets to curious tourists.

Shaker basket, ash splint, tightly woven, New England, late nineteenth century, 8½″ long x 7″ to top of handle, splayed sides, checker work bottom.

These baskets were skillfully woven but their light weight limits their use.

Shaker wool gathering basket, New England, late nineteenth century, grip handles, wire band holding thick splint, 29½″ x 23″ x 11″ tall, uncommonly found form.

Tightly made gathering basket, probably Shaker, woven around a mold, nineteenth century, oak splint, 9″ diameter x 11″ to top of handle. This is a larger and more functional version of the miniature Shaker basket described previously.

The raised bottom, tight weave, rigid handle, and use of a mold are characteristics often found on Shaker-made baskets. This is a similar example of a form used for eggs, produce, or as a utility basket.

Shaker "feather" type basket, New England, nineteenth century, painted, woven over a mold. The handle of the basket is set inside the rim of the lid. This allows the lid to slide up and down the handle with little difficulty.

If feathers were stored in the basket, they could be easily removed with few able to escape by blowing away.

Another tightly woven Shaker "feather" basket in a slightly different form. This basket was also woven over a wooden mold. The handle has been separated from the basket at some point.

"Feather" type basket, Shaker-made, New England, nineteenth century, stained a deep brown, woven over a mold.

Another Shaker-made "feather" basket, ash splint, woven over a mold, 9″ diameter x 11″ high to top of the handle.

The size of this basket would prohibit it from holding too many feathers.

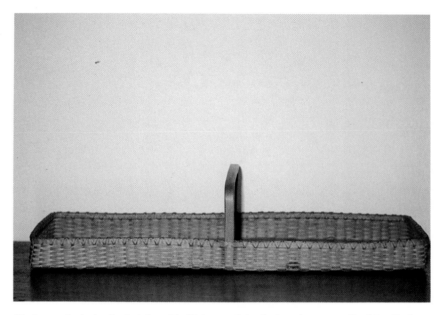

Shaker apple drying basket, found in Maine, ca. late nineteenth century, fixed handle from oak splint, 33½″ long x 12″ wide x 7½″ high to top of handle.

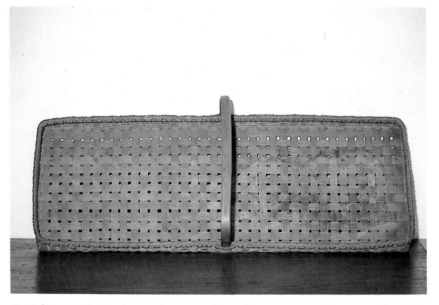

If a basket was designed to perform a specific task, some traces of heavy use should be evident. The interior of this example is heavily stained from contact with apples.

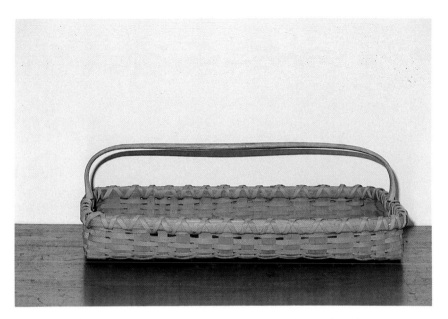

Rectangular herb gathering basket, fixed handle running the length of the basket, cross or "x" bound rim, possibly Shaker, 26″ x 14″ x 8″ tall to top of handle.

Shaker storage box, ca. early twentieth century, New England, woven poplar with silk decorative ribbon, 4″ x 8″ x 3½″ tall.

Unusual Shaker carrier for bringing berries in from field, late nineteenth-early twentieth century, found in Ohio, drop or swing handle of wire with maple grip.

The eight individual berry baskets are made from thickly cut oak splint and tacked together.

Double rim, thick oak splint, wire drop handle.

Oblong market basket, possibly Shaker-made, New England, two splint "runners" on the bottom, double wrapped rim, 11″ tall x 14″ across.

Splint field basket, open weave on bottom that allowed debris to fall through, found in Illinois, late nineteenth-early twentieth century.

The basket has a diameter of 28″ and was found in a "boutique" in a small central Illinois community. Finding an exceptional country antique in an unlikely location has been discussed previously. It was purchases like this one that kept us searching for baskets in even more unlikely places for at least two years. To date we have never found another one.

The splint basket was made with six hickory branches ranging in size from 1″ to 2″ in diameter. The oak splint was woven between them.

Tobacco market basket, commonly found in Virginia and the Carolinas, ca. early twentieth century, 36″ x 48″.

Oak splint bed mat, checker work construction, found in Virginia, ca. mid-nineteenth century.

We have only seen one other bed mat and that was similar in form and construction to this example, but had a pine frame. The mat was placed on top of the ropes and the mattress or a homespun bag filled with corn shucks was placed on the mat.

Collectors of country baskets generally have not had to concern themselves with determining whether a basket was made in Europe or America. The biggest difficulty has been in identifying Indian-made baskets. This utility or gathering basket is an import.

The handle is an unusually thick piece of wood made from a branch or small limb. It runs down the side of the basket and becomes a "foot" that keeps the bottom of the basket off of the ground.

Field or gathering basket, uncommon form, late nineteenth century, white oak splint, found in northeastern United States.

Fruit gathering basket, New York State, ca. late nineteenth century, oak splint, found in northeastern United States.

The basket was strapped on like a tool belt with a rope passing through the bows on the front of the basket and around the apple picker's waist. The "kicked in" back was designed for a picker who ate a lot of apples.

Apple drying basket, oak splint, pine frame, late nineteenth century, 38″ x 14″ x 3½″ deep.

The pine frame of the basket is mortised together rather than nailed or dovetailed.

Oak splint winnowing basket, pine hoop or frame, carved handles, mid-to late nineteenth century, New England.

The basket has a diameter of 27″ with an open weave bottom.

The hoop is made of pine and is 6″ wide.

The two hand carved handles are lashed with splint to the sides of the hoop.

Footed storage or drying basket, New England, ca. first half of the nineteenth century, 30″ x 14″ x 12″.

It is uncommon to find a basket with mortise and tenon construction. Each rib or framing piece is mortised and secured with a wooden pin. The four end posts are extended and serve as a "foot" that elevates the bottom of the basket and allows air to circulate.

The weaving is a simple "over and under" pattern utilizing the frame or ribs of the basket. The frame and end posts are constructed of walnut.

White oak splint berry baskets, late nineteenth century, found in New Jersey, 4½" diameter x 7" to top of handle. In the early 1970's an advertisement in the *Maine Antiques Digest* offered a supply of berry baskets that had been uncovered in a warehouse in New Jersey. The baskets were designed to be filled with strawberries and delivered to restaurants in New York City for individual servings.

Oak splint mellon basket, ca. late nineteenth century, found in Virginia.

Tightly woven buttocks basket, unusually small splint, southeastern United States, late nineteenth century.

Oak splint utility or market basket, checker work bottom, uncommonly intricate weaving pattern on handle, found in southeast United States, late nineteenth-early twentieth century.

Oak splint market or utility basket, fairly common form, early twentieth century, southeastern United States.

Miniature mellon basket, oak splint, dark patina, found in southern Indiana.

This basket was probably part of a nest of three or four mellon baskets. It could have been used by a child for gathering eggs. The basket measures 5½" end to end and 4½" to the top of the handle. The ribs were carved from white oak and the handle was tightly "x" bound to the rim.

White oak utility basket, rib construction, handle carved from a thick piece of oak splint, southeastern United States, early twentieth century.

Splint mending or sewing basket, round mouth tapering to square bottom, 11″ to top of handle, 10″ diameter, 6″ x 6″ bottom.

Market or utility basket, probably New England, late nineteenth century, white oak splint, 13″ to top of handle, 14″ diameter at mouth, 15½″ in length, rib construction.

A basket with a specially woven handle rather than a carved piece of splint probably was a gift or a special order.

Utility or egg basket, square bottom with round mouth, oak splint, probably midwestern, ca. late nineteenth century, 9″ to top of handle, diameter of 7″.

Storage basket, ash splint, tightly woven around a wooden mold, early twentieth century, New England, oval mouth and rectanglar bottom.

Carved bow handles, held in place between double rim and notched.

Open weave, checker work bottom.

Splint storage basket, 8″ long x 5″ wide x 4″ deep, no handles, wrapped rim.

Checker work open weave bottom of splint storage basket.

White oak splint market basket, buttocks form, found in Pennsylvania, ca. 1900, twisted splint handle for strength, 28" end to end, 13" to top of the handle.

Miniature white oak market basket, 11″ end to end, 8″ to top of the handle, buttocks form, ca. 1900, twisted splint handle.

Market or storage basket, white oak splint, ca. early twentieth century, 25″ long x 20″ to top of the handle. Baskets in this form were used to take chickens or ducks to market. A basket filled with a live duck would also be filled with droppings. This basket is reasonably clean on the inside and carries no mementoes from its former tenants.

Only one end of the market or storage basket has a hinged lid.

The technique used to reinforce the handle is called a "folded square". The handle is made of twisted splint.

Mending or sewing basket, demi-john bottom, oak splint, 9″ diameter, bow handles, New England, late nineteenth century.

The bowed handle is held by the rim and notched. The rim is double or "x" bound.

Buttocks basket, white oak splint, rib construction, 9″ to top of handle x 10″ across.

Buttocks basket, oak and ash splint, rib construction, early twentieth century.

This is another example of the "folded square" to secure the handle to the rim of the basket.

Splint gathering basket, oval mouth and rectangular bottom, 21″ end to end and 11″ across, "x" bound rim, open weave bottom, New England, ca. late nineteenth century.

Buttocks basket, oak splint, rib construction, probably midwestern, late nineteenth century.

Willow basket, used for gathering eggs or small produce, found in Pennsylvania, probably early twentieth century. Weavers made of willow could also be called osiers or rods. The sides of the basket are held tightly to the rim by the "folded square".

Mellon basket, rib construction, oak splint, found in Ohio, 7½″ across x 8″ to top of handle.

Contemporary white oak buttocks basket. When this basket acquires a patina through exposure to light, air, weather, and use it will be impossible to distinguish it from a basket made a century earlier.

Tightly woven miniature mellon basket, ash splint, great patina, rib construction, "x" bound rim, found in Pennsylvania, nineteenth century, 5″ end to end x 4½″ to top of handle. We bought this basket at Shupp's Grove near Adamstown, Pennsylvania for $80.00 in 1977.

Rye straw storage basket, "bee hive" form, coiled construction, southeastern United States, early twentieth century. The individual coils are held together by strips of oak splint.

Flower or herb gathering basket, ca. twentieth century, machine cut oak splint, open weave bottom. This basket was factory made and held together with nails. The splint is identical in size and depth with no tool marks or man-made imperfections. This basket form is still being produced in large quantities.

Rye straw utility basket, hickory handle, 11″ diameter x 13″ to top of handle, uncommon form. The typical rye straw basket that collectors find is a bread or dough rising basket. The majority of the rye straw baskets were made in Pennsylvania. In recent years there have been a great many rye straw baskets in various forms reproduced. Take special note of the patina on the oak splint that binds the coils of rye straw on any basket you may be offered.

Wall or half basket, small branch used for a handle, probably an egg basket, nineteenth century, crudely executed. Compare this example with the imported "footed" basket that was previously described and you will see some striking similarities.

The bottom was woven in a checker work pattern with thickly cut splint.

The handle is held to the basket by the finely cut weavers.

White oak half basket, found in Indiana, ca. early twentieth century.

Exceptionally well made half basket, tightly woven oak splint, New England, nineteenth century, rib construction.

White oak half basket, "oriole" form with unusually deep storage area, rib construction with dyed weavers, probably from Kentucky or Tennessee, nineteenth century.

Bobbin or comb basket, probably Indian-made, New England, late nineteenth century, painted green, 6″ across x 7″ to top of splint hook for hanging. A comb basket was hung on a wall with a small mirror propped against the back. Shaving brushes, razors, or combs could also be stored in the basket. Bobbins were wooden cylinders or spindles on which yarn or thread was stored. The basket was hung on a loom post and bobbins were placed inside.

The basket is made from ½″ wide pieces of splint. The finely cut splint strips on the upper portion are designed to hold the basket together. It carries several coats of paint.

Miniature white oak basket, 3″ diameter x 4″ to top of handle, purchased in West Virginia, made in the mid-1970's.

Shaker splint storage basket for table, fine weavers with wide splint checker work bottom, heart shaped bow handles, 14″ diameter at mouth x 8½″ x 9½″ at bottom x 6″ to rim.

Shaker miniature basket, round with extremely fine weavers and two bow handles, unusual cloverleaf design woven on bottom, probably from Sabbathday Lake, Maine, 5½″ diameter x 2½″ to rim.

Shaker sewing basket, 10″ diameter at mouth x 6″ square bottom x 4½″ to rim, the strawberry is filled with ground pumice for sharpening needles, four woven pockets for sewing materials.

Oblong splint basket, New England, 14″ x 8½″ x 11″ to top of the handle, probably a market basket, possibly Shaker-made.

Miniature buttocks basket, remnants of green paint, 8″ end to end, oak splint, New England.

Market basket, machine cut oak splint, thick splint handle, ca. first half of the twentieth century.

The handle is bound to the sides of the basket. These baskets were made in large quantities and are not difficult to find. Often they are equally as expensive as a basket made a century earlier.

Splint egg basket, found in New England, possibly Shaker, colored with a grey "wash", 9″ to top of the handle x 5½″ diameter.

Splint egg basket, found in New England, possibly Shaker, colored with a deep red stain. 11″ to top of handle x 7½″ diameter.

Rectangular splint market basket, nicely carved handle, double wrapped rim, New England, 19½″ x 12½″ x 6½″ to rim.

Bulbous round basket, oak splint with fixed handle, demi-john bottom, possibly Shaker, 12½″ diameter 15¼″ to top of handle, nineteenth century.

Gathering or egg basket, demi-john bottom, ash splint, New England, nineteenth century.

FINAL EXAMINATION

It is important that after you have digested such a significant work as this, you have the opportunity to exhibit your knowledge. We have created a testing instrument that will accurately assess your appreciation of American country baskets.

This test is an important step in your quest to become an expert in the field. If you fail, the highest status you may attain is "authority". That title will only get you speaking engagements at family reunions. To be an expert you must pass this examination *and* have your own slides. Your future is in the balance. If you do not do well, don't blame us.

Directions:

Read each question carefully and select an answer that appears to be correct. When you go to the first speaking engagement, don't forget to take an extra bulb for the slide projector and enough drop cord.

1. What are two terms used to describe the type of handle on this basket?

2. The weavers in the basket are made of _____.
   a. rattan
   b. oak splint
   c. ash splint
   d. walnut

3. Where was this basket made?

4. True   False   The basket has a turned wooden bottom.

5. This basket
    a. has a "drop" handle
    b. was woven over a mold
    c. is made with rattan
    d. a & c are both correct

6. This basket is made of
   a. rattan
   b. oak splint
   c. ash splint
   d. walnut

7. It was used
   a. to seperate curds from whey
   b. for gathering produce
   c. for gathering herbs or flowers
   d. for all of the above

8. True   False   The bottom of the basket was woven in a checker work pattern.

9. This basket dates from about
   a. 1800-1840
   b. 1860-1875
   c. 1880-early 1900's

10. It was made by_____in New England.

11. It is made with _____.
    a. rattan
    b. ash splint
    c. oak splint
    d. woven poplar

12. This is a _____ basket.

13. If this basket had a diameter of 26″ and was in good repair, what would be its approximate market value?

14. Name two terms that describe the bottom of this basket.

15. True   False   This basket was woven over a basket mold.

16. Which of the terms below describe the rim of this basket?
    _____"x" bound
    _____a folded square
    _____double bound
    _____single wrapped

17. This basket handle could also be called a _____.

18. True   False   This basket appears to have been factory made in the late nineteenth century.

19. This is a _____ basket.

20. True   False   It probably dates from prior to 1850.

21. Would "rib construction" accurately describe this basket?
    yes   no

22. This basket could be called a "wall" basket or a
    "_____" basket.

23. A close inspection of this basket would suggest that the splint was machine cut rather than prepared by hand.

                yes   no

24. Which of the statements below are true?

    _____The basket was made by American Indians.

    _____The basket dates after 1880.

    _____The basket is an import.

25. Check the items below that you are going to take on your first speaking engagement.

    _____extra bulb for the projector

    _____drop cord (extra)

    _____this book for reference

    _____car keys

    _____mother-in-law (or mother)

Answers

1. swing or drop
2. a. rattan
3. Nantucket, Mass.
4. True
5. b. was woven over a mold
6. b. oak splint
7. c. for gathering herbs or flowers
8. true
9. c. 1880-1900's
10. the Shakers
11. d. woven poplar
12. "cheese"
13. $400.00-600.00
14. demi-john or "kicked in"
15. true
16. single wrapped
17. bow
18. false
19. buttocks
20. false
21. yes
22. half
23. yes
24. The basket was made by American Indians. The basket dates after 1880.
25. You are absolutely correct.

Scoring Scale

22-25 correct—No doubt about it, you are a national authority.

18-21 correct—If you buy another copy of this book, you have the potential to be a national authority.

14-17 correct—Sell the extra bulb for the projector, the drop cord, and give your slides away. It's over.

10-13— You have embarrassed us and your family. Turn out the lights.

Price Guide

Page

7 Utility basket $450.00-500.00
8 Storage basket $350.00-375.00
11 Splint knife and fork
    basket $275.00-300.00
12 Gathering basket $125.00-150.00
    Buttocks basket $200.00-275.00
13 Utility basket $100.00-135.00
    Garden basket $130.00-150.00
14 Utility basket $250.00-325.00
15 Storage basket $75.00-100.00
16 Indian-made storage basket $175.00
17 Storage basket $250.00-350.00
19 Cheese basket $575.00-650.00
20 Shaker cheese basket...$750.00-900.00
21 Windsor-type cheese
    ladder $500.00-575.00
22 Pine cheese ladder $30.00-45.00
23 Cheese weave drying
    basket $450.00-525.00
24 Painted oak splint
    basket $700.00-900.00
26 Market basket $175.00-225.00
27 Machine-cut splint $15.00-20.00
    Storage basket $125.00-150.00
28 Buttocks basket $140.00-175.00
29 Storage basket $150.00-185.00
30 Swing handled
    basket $550.00-625.00
33 Swing handled
    basket $500.00-575.00
    "Lightship" basket . $750.00-825.00
36 Swing handled splint
    basket $350.00-425.00
37 Swing handled oak splint
    basket $325.00-375.00
38 Swing handled oak splint
    basket $400.00-450.00
40 Miniature swing handled
    basket $500.00-600.00
44 White oak splint
    basket $350.00-375.00
47 Shaker double swing handled market
    basket $450.00-575.00
    Shaker miniature
    basket $625.00-675.00

48 Ash splint Shaker
    basket $500.00-600.00
49 Shaker wool gathering
    basket $425.00-450.00
50 Gathering basket $225.00-300.00
51 Utility basket $200.00-225.00
52 Shaker "feather" type
    basket $400.00-475.00
54 Shaker "feather" type
    basket $400.00-500.00
55 Shaker "feather" type
    basket $400.00-500.00
56 Shaker "feather" type
    basket $375.00-450.00
58 Shaker apple drying
    basket $800.00-1,100.00
59 Herb gathering
    basket $400.00-475.00
    Shaker dresser box ... $50.00-75.00
60 Shaker carrier $1,100.00-1,300.00
62 Market basket $250.00-275.00
63 Field splint basket $600.00-700.00
64 Tobacco market basket .. $50.00-65.00
65 Oak splint bed mat $450.00-550.00
66 Imported utility basket ... $75.00-85.00
67 Field basket $250.00-285.00
68 Fruit gathering
    basket $425.00-500.00
70 Apple drying basket ... $525.00-575.00
72 Oak splint winnowing
    basket $600.00-675.00
74 Footed storage
    basket $550.00-650.00
76 Berry baskets ...... $95.00-120.00 each
77 Mellon basket $85.00-100.00
    Buttocks basket $200.00-225.00
78 Utility basket $150.00-200.00
    Market basket $65.00-75.00
79 Miniature mellon
    basket $200.00-225.00
80 Utility basket $150.00-200.00
    Splint mending
    basket $150.00-185.00
81 Market basket $150.00-200.00
    Utility basket $150.00-185.00

Bibliography

We have made an effort below to provide a list of reference books we frequently call upon when a question about baskets arises. Modesty has not forbid us from including two of our own works in the list. The magazine, *Antique Collecting,* had an exceptional special basket issue in June, 1978. The publication, originally from Ephrata, Pennsylvania, is no longer in operation.

Larason, Lew, *Basket Collector's Book*, Scorpio Publications, 1978.

Lasansky, Jeannette, *Willow, Oak, and Rye*, Union Co. Oral Traditions Project, 1978.

Raycraft, Don and Carol, *Country Basket*s, Wallace-Homestead Book Co., 1976.

Raycraft, Don and Carol, *The Basket Book*, Collector Books, 1981.

Seeler, Katherine and Edgar, *Nantucket Lightship Baskets*, Deermouse Press, 1972.

Teleki, Gloria, *The Baskets of Rural America*, Dutton, 1975.